DUSIE WITHDRAWN

Girls as Constructors
in the Early Years

185 856 0020

i

Girls as Constructors in the Early Years

Promoting equal opportunites in maths, science and technology

Carol Ross and Naima Browne

Trentham Books

First published in 1993 by Trentham Books Limited

Trentham Books Limited
Westview House
734 London Road
Oakhill
Stoke-on-Trent
Staffordshire
England ST4 5NP

British Library Cataloguing Publication Data
A catalogue record for this book is available from the British Library.

ISBN: 1 85856 002 0

Designed and typeset by Trentham Print Design Limited
and printed by Bemrose Shafron Limited, Chester.

Contents

INTRODUCTION:
Girls and construction play
— why does it matter?

Maths, science and technology form a major part of the National Curriculum. However, despite the emphasis that has been placed on promoting maths, science and technology amongst girls, recent statistics show that these areas are still heavily dominated by boys (21.9 percent of boys and only 9.2 percent of girls leaving school in 1987 had 'O' level passes in physics and 17.1 percent of boys as against 4.5 percent of girls had 'O' level passes in Design Technology). (*DES Statistical Bulletin: *English School Leavers* 1986-1987)

Girls form a disproportionately small percentage of students opting for these and related subjects at 'A' level and in Higher Education. Jobs in areas involving maths, science and technology are dominated by men. Women form a disproportionately low percentage of this workforce.

Differences in girls' and boys' involvement in maths, science and technology is not confined to 16 year olds but is already evident amongst very young children in nursery and infant classrooms. Observations of children in early years classrooms reveal that girls and boys are often engaged in quite different sorts of activities or use resources in different ways (see chart series A).

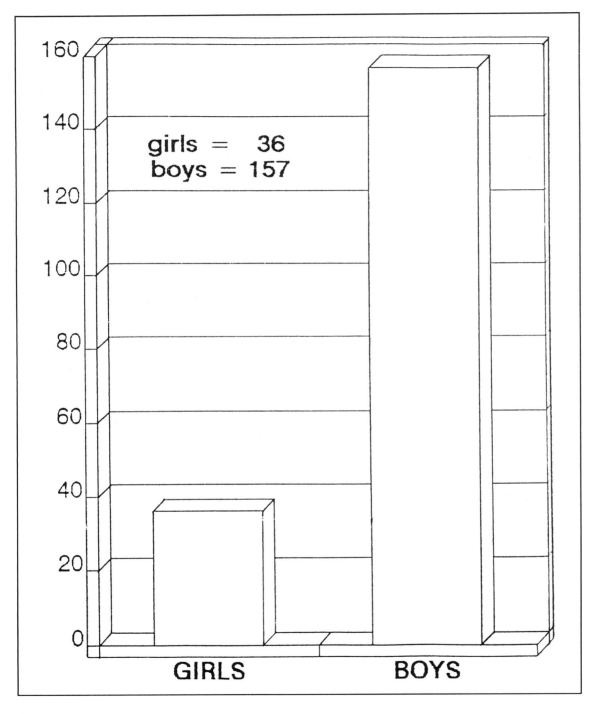

girls = 36
boys = 157

GIRLS   **BOYS**

Chart Series A
CONSTRUCTION ACTIVITIES
Observation Period:
6 hrs 10 mins.
No. of Nurseries
observed :3
Number of Girls and Boys Engaged in Construction Play

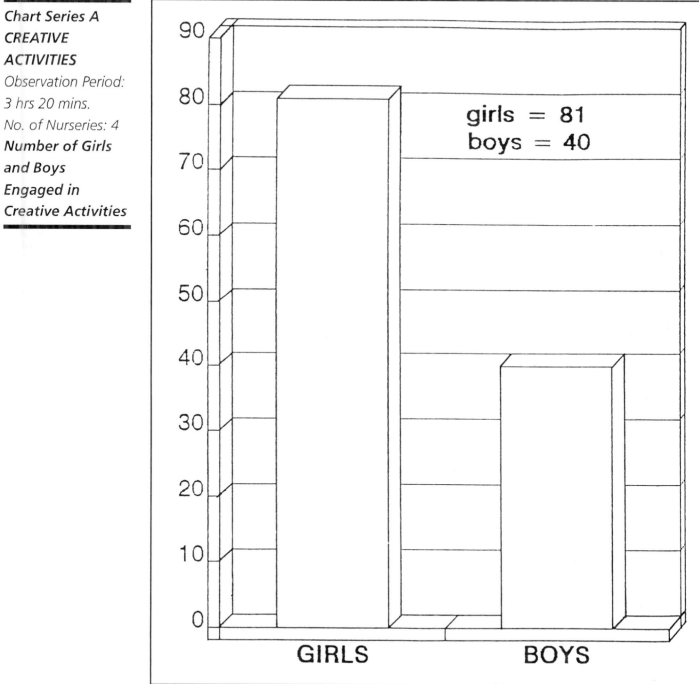

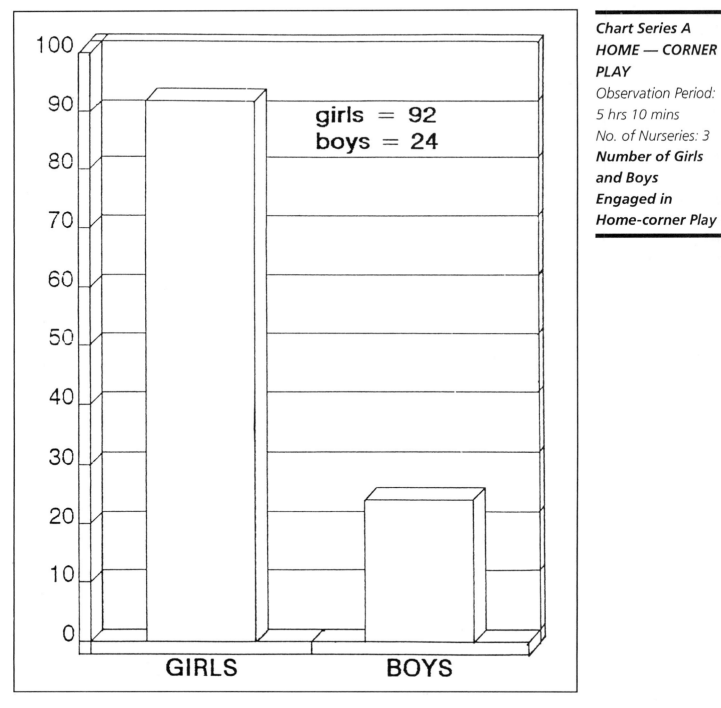

girls = 92
boys = 24

Chart Series A
***HOME — CORNER
PLAY***
*Observation Period:
5 hrs 10 mins*
No. of Nurseries: 3
**Number of Girls
and Boys
Engaged in
Home-corner Play**

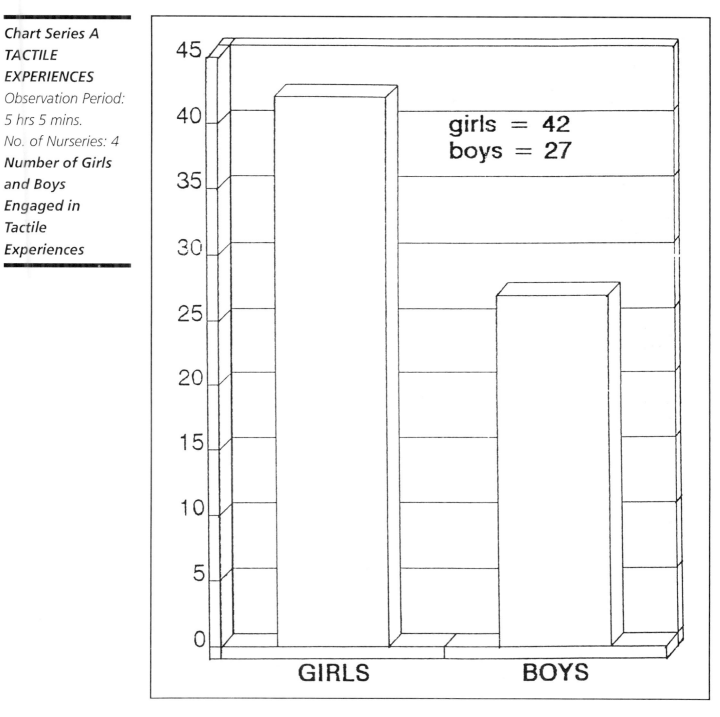

Chart Series A
TACTILE
EXPERIENCES
Observation Period:
5 hrs 5 mins.
No. of Nurseries: 4
Number of Girls
and Boys
Engaged in
Tactile
Experiences

girls = 42
boys = 27

GIRLS   BOYS

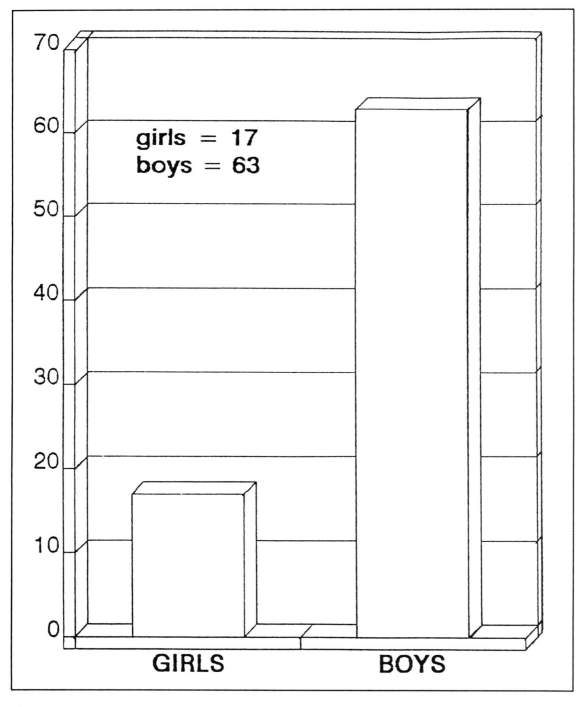

girls = 17
boys = 63

GIRLS   BOYS

**Chart Series A
'SMALL WORLD'**
*Observation Period:
4 hrs 55 mins.
No. of Nurseries: 3*
**Number of Girls
and Boys
Engaged in 'Small
World' Play**

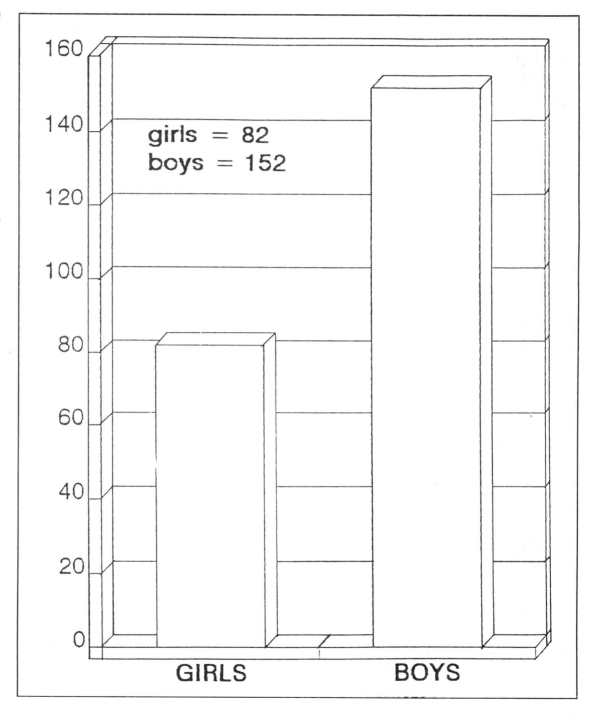

It is important to tackle inequalities in educational experiences at this early stage. Many schools are working at developing maths, science and design and technology in the early years as required by the National Curriculum. However, research — and our own experiences —has shown that unless specific strategies are adopted, gender, race and social class can affect children's learning in various areas of the curriculum, and Early Years teachers have expressed concern over the resulting imbalances in the development of skills and interests in their pupils.

Many teachers have observed the reticence of some girls to enter into constructional activities. Teachers often comment that girls commonly seem overly worried about 'getting it right' and may be unwilling to undertake tasks they're unsure of. These feelings may well influence girls' problem-solving skills and their ability to design experiments and to hypothesise (which involves the willingness to take intellectual 'risks') and may lead to loss of confidence and interest at this very early stage.

There is a strong feeling in education that it is vital for schools to take positive steps to ensure that girls' learning in these areas does not lag behind that of boys. This means finding ways to ensure that girls develop a solid foundation of relevant concepts, skills and positive attitudes in the crucial early years so that they're not hindered later on in terms of job opportunities.

We have been working in Islington schools on a project initially supported by the ILEA Sex Equality Fund and then by Islington Education Department since April 1990. We have focused on constructional play in early years classrooms, examining the extent of girls' involvement in this area and developing practical strategies to promote equal opportunities. We identified constructional play because these activities relate directly to mathematical, scientific and design technology skills (see chart B) and also because these are often free-choice activities, left to the child to determine whether and how they are pursued.

This handbook is the outcome of our work. It contains three main sections: the issues highlighted by the project about girls in relation to constructional activities: specific strategies for working with girls; and INSET ideas to facilitate exploring your own classroom context.

An analysis of construction play illustrates how such activities relate to specific targets in the National Curriculum

SCIENCE

eg. Types and uses of materials
Forces
Scientific process
(Exploration,
investigation, reporting,
responding)

MATHS

eg.   Measurement
Shape and Space
Types of Movement

CONSTRUCTIONAL
ACTIVITIES

Junk Modelling
Woodwork
Paper Engineering
Mobilo
Lego / Duplo
Giant builder etc.

Technology

eg.   Design and making
Forces and Energy
Practical problem solving
Explorations of possible
solutions

Promoting constructional activities in the early years can help girls become confident and competent later on.

SECTION 1

Girls and constructional activities
Issues highlighted by the project

During the course of the project certain issues were raised which relate to girls' levels of involvement in construction play and the quality of their learning.

The first is that girls do not use construction and mechanical toys as often as boys choose to. This finding is well documented.

Children from a very young age seem to identify activities in a gender-related way ('girls' toys' and 'boys' toys'). One effect of this can be that children might not venture into areas/activities which they have identified as 'belonging' to the other sex.

Children may feel that they are not entitled to an activity/classroom area if they perceive it as lying outside their 'gender domain'.

Children who venture outside their 'gender domain' might become easily discouraged and need extra support, even those who operate with a high degree of confidence and independence elsewhere.

We start from the premise that girls, like boys, have the necessary abilities and capacities to perform competently in spatial, mechanical and technological activities.

'Female' activities (such as dress-making, cooking, making cardboard dolls' houses and furniture, paper bags and baskets) all involve a process of conceptualising a finished product, considering how to construct it from a range of non-specific components, and executing the plan and modifying it as necessary. We argue, therefore, that children's attitudes and approaches to activities are dependent on a sense of entitlement and confidence, rather than simply on possessing a particular 'type' of knowledge and aptitude.

In any field, an individual's progress and ability to function effectively in a challenging situation involves a willingness to take risks and tolerate uncertainty. It is easier for children to take risks in areas where they feel confident. A feeling of lack of 'entitlement' and lower involvement in constructional activities can undermine girls' confidence and make it harder for them to take 'risks' and experiment. This in turn affects the development of new skills and understandings. Lower levels of involvement in construction activities can prevent girls from making the link between the skills and concepts learnt in a familiar context and those required in an unfamiliar context and so impair their ability to transfer skills and knowledge and develop 'flexible' thinking. For example, many girls are confident about assembling jigsaw puzzles, which involve concepts of shape and spatial arrangement, yet may be unsure how to use con-

struction toys which require similar concepts.

Additionally, many 'girls' games' are rule-dominated (such as jigsaw puzzles, skipping, hopscotch) whereas construction play and other 'boys' games' are open-ended and operate in the realm of ambiguity (laying out a train-track, football, creating lego models). This may increase the sense of insecurity many girls exhibit over activities of this kind.

In order to begin to investigate the ways children's experiences of school can be affected by their gender, we visited a number of early years classrooms and began focusing on the following questions:

What were the children playing with?

How were they using equipment, toys and space?

In which sorts of activities were they developing interest and skill?

We began by photographing different areas and equipment in classrooms when they were not in use. Then we used these photos as a way to interview the children about what they played with, how they played with it, who else played with it and what they were and were not interested in. We were careful never to talk in terms of 'boys' and 'girls' — although the children did. Some intriguing information came out of these taped discussions:

1. Whenever a boy identified an activity he enjoyed or something he played with, we asked who else in the class like to do likewise. The boy would then list all the other boys in the class and only when pressed would mention any girls.

2. All the boys were very enthusiastic about the photo of the lego table. Few girls said they played with it, and then only when pressed, and some girls said they didn't like lego at all. (Teachers said that in fact the boys usually dominate the lego table.)

3. Most children described lego as being used to make cars and houses — and named boys as making cars and girls as making houses.

   Marissa: *I make houses of lego... Espidito, Scott and Keith make cars and we make houses.*

4. Some girls said they didn't like to use lego because other children took over whenever they had difficulty making the bricks stick together.

5. Boys described using the 'home comer' in a variety of ways — they played 'dogs', 'knightrider', 'cars' and 'mummies and daddies'. Girls described only playing 'house':

   We play shopping and we set the table.
   I'm the mummy and she's the sister.
   I like to play with the dolls.

From the interviews, it appeared that boys and girls may not only choose different sorts of activities but may even use the same activities differently.

We decided to choose a construction activity (Lego) and observe the children while they worked. Teachers assigned equal numbers of girls and boys to the lego table. Some of the behaviour of girls was very different from most of the boys'. These are some things we consistently observed:

☐ All the boys assumed that the girls would make houses. For example, Scott and Benji asked Amy and Rosie if they wanted the 'window' bricks for their houses before they even began building. In another similar incident, one girl replied 'I'm not making a house... Oh, I guess I will'.

☐ All the girls observed took a very limited approach to using the lego (green base for floor, edged with one row of bricks for walls and some basic 'tables' and 'chairs').

☐ The boys used the lego in much more sophisticated ways, making more use of it as a medium, exploiting its three-dimensional properties (e.g. balance, capacity for movement, potential for complexity of configuration, etc).

☐ Girls often brought 'play people' over to the table to use as dolls, and used their lego houses as a prop for social play about families at home.

☐ Boys usually played briefly and noisily (with sound effects) with each car, aeroplane, gun they made from lego, then changed the construction into something else. There was a constant process of making and remaking lego constructions.

☐ Girls played 'house' with each other, constantly interacting as an intrinsic part of the play.

☐ Boys played with their constructions on their own.

☐ When provided with a place to display lego models, the girls were more concerned to complete and display their models, the boys less concerned with their 'end product'.

☐ After two sessions at the lego table, girls began to use the lego much more often (without us). Some girls even asked the teachers to set it out for them.

We extended our observations to a second construction activity and chose the train set. As soon as we sat at the train table (usually boy-dominated) several things happened:

☐ Girls were anxious to play at the train table.

☐ The girls were awkward and unsure about how to play with the trains.

☐ By bringing 'play people' over to the table and having them hit by trains, they were able to set up a 'hospital' and thus change the activity into social play concerned with looking after people.

☐ When some boys joined this table later on, they 'knew' exactly how to play with the trains and the game hotted up.

We went on to look at a range of other constructional and technological activities with other teachers:

Woodwork

Balsa wood shapes, glue, hammers, rails, paints and brushes were provided.

As Christmas was approaching, the children were given a 'toy' theme and invited to make models of the toys they'd like to get for Christmas. Most children, girls as well as boys, made cars, aeroplanes and helicopters.

The children were asked about the toys they made and if they'd enjoy playing with them. Many girls said the cars and aeroplanes they made were for their brothers, even though they had been asked initially to make the toys for themselves.

Clearing up time tended to reveal pronounced gender role differences. We often observed that most of the girls took responsibility and worked in an efficient way, while half the boys always wandered around aimlessly or walked about without clearing up.

Junk Modelling

Teachers observed that boys make bigger models. They'd go in search of larger boxes than those set out to choose from. They made mostly robots and spaceships.

The girls' models were on a smaller scale, but more interesting in their attention to details such as symmetry and pattern. They often didn't say that their models were a particular thing, but regarded them in a purely design sense.

New Materials

Several teachers tried giving the girls in their class material (duplex) which was new to the class. The girls were unwilling to try to use it without their teacher to help them begin to play with it.

Physical Play

Alongside observing classrooms, we also began looking at what happens in the playground. One important thing to emerge from this work was how differently girls and boys used the playground in terms of utilising space, making noise, physical activity and social behaviour.

We consider this relevant to children's three-dimensional and spatial awareness and that it corresponds to the gender differences concerning construction play we were finding the classroom.

Questions Highlighted

As a result of our investigations, we ended up with some very large questions which are central to the quality of children's learning experiences:

Are girls getting less opportunities to develop mechanical, manipulation and spatial skills to the same extent that boys do, because they're dominated by social play which influences their choice of activity and the strategies they employ in those activities?

Does feeling less entitled than boys to certain activities hold girls back in their development of skills and interests?

To what extent is the teacher a role model in terms of gender?

What are the educational implications of how girls and boys appear to use materials differently?

How can girls be helped to extend their participation (and ability) in constructional and physical activities which develop manipulative, mechanical and spatial skills?

Could it be that at some level girls and boys are concerned with quite different learning processes — boys with the process of doing and making, and girls with the process of social interaction?

And does a focus on social intercourse mean that girls may be more aware of the ways others react to them and feel about things?

Do they therefore feel a greater need to please the teacher?

Does this mean they're less free to explore the process of doing and making and more bound to producing finished products?

Are there differences in the ways boys and girls make a task 'their own'?

If boys are willing to take more risks in their play, what are the learning implications?

Why might girls be worried about experimenting with a new medium?

Did the girls see the construction activity as the province of boys?

If an activity is viewed as the girls' province, are boys willing to experiment?

How much does the question of 'entitlement' enter into the issue, for both girls and boys?

How transferable are skills relating to three-dimensional activities? (Does the fact that many boys may have more experience with other types of 3D materials help them in these tasks?)

How do girls/boys experiment with the material? What are the apparent differences in approach etc? What would be the effect of extra practice for the girls?

How do girls/boys view construction materials in terms of what can be made? Does perceiving lego and other such material as being for making cars, etc, mean that girls see these as not for them?

These are the sorts of questions which became the basis for the next phase of the project. This was to begin developing specific strategies to help increase the access of girls to constructional activities. Ideas for practice arose through responding to data from our classroom observations. We devised and trialled various methods, then observed and refined them further. The next section of this handbook is a collection of the strategies and approaches which have emerged from this process.

SECTION 2

Increasing Girls' Access to Construction Activities
Practical strategies and approaches

In your classroom, are you concerned that:

☐ Some girls won't take risks' within construction activities?

☐ Girls aren't transferring their skills in other areas to construction activities?

☐ Some girls have had very little experience with construction toys?

☐ Even when they do use the construction toys, girls mainly make a very limited range of models?

The following pages outline strategies which we have trialled in response to teachers' concern that girls in their classroom are not developing skills and interest in constructional activities.

I You like the things that you're good at
You're good at the things you like

Children who aren't confident about an activity may continually avoid engaging in it by 'deciding' that they don't like it.

Observations in nursery and infant classrooms show that girls often reject constructional play as an option, on the grounds that 'it's boring' or they don't like it. In early years classrooms where children are able to make independent choices about what they play with, it can be difficult for teachers to break the cycle. Therefore, a first step is to be alert to the *avoidance tactics* which girls may employ.

Picking up the clues

☐ *I don't want to play with lego. I don't like it.* — Infant girl.

☐ Teacher: *Why don't you want to play with the Rio Click?*
Girl: *It's boring.*

☐ *These six girls are constantly avioding challenge by focusing on a fringe activity, such as decorating the materials.*
— Infant Teacher

☐ *A group of girls in my class really enjoy working with me, unless I'm trying to get them involved in a constructional activity. Then they just sit. there.*
— Infant Teacher.

One useful way to help girls overcome their reluctance to engage in constructional play is to begin with a familiar area and move gradually into 'unfamiliar territory' (there are two examples of this approach on the following pages).

a: Outline of case study I: Movement

Principles:

☐ Starting with activities in which girls are confident, competent and interested.

☐ Broadening their interests and skills.

☐ Introducing new concepts, skills, etc. in small stages, to ensure that the children remain confident.

Aims:

investigating types of movement
Designing and marking
Practical problem solving/exploring possible solutions
Exploring types and uses of materials.

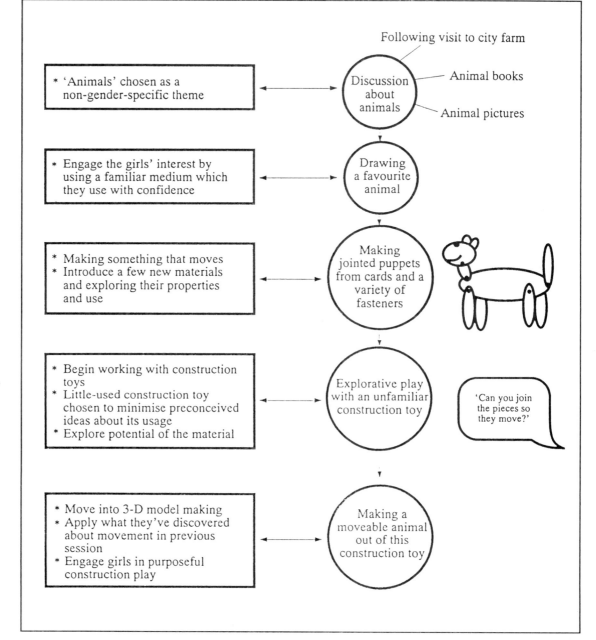

* 'Animals' chosen as a non-gender-specific theme

↔ Discussion about animals — Following visit to city farm — Animal books — Animal pictures

* Engage the girls' interest by using a familiar medium which they use with confidence

↔ Drawing a favourite animal

* Making something that moves
* Introduce a few new materials and exploring their properties and use

↔ Making jointed puppets from cards and a variety of fasteners

* Begin working with construction toys
* Little-used construction toy chosen to minimise preconceived ideas about its usage
* Explore potential of the material

↔ Explorative play with an unfamiliar construction toy

'Can you join the pieces so they move?'

* Move into 3-D model making
* Apply what they've discovered about movement in previous session
* Engage girls in purposeful construction play

↔ Making a moveable animal out of this construction toy

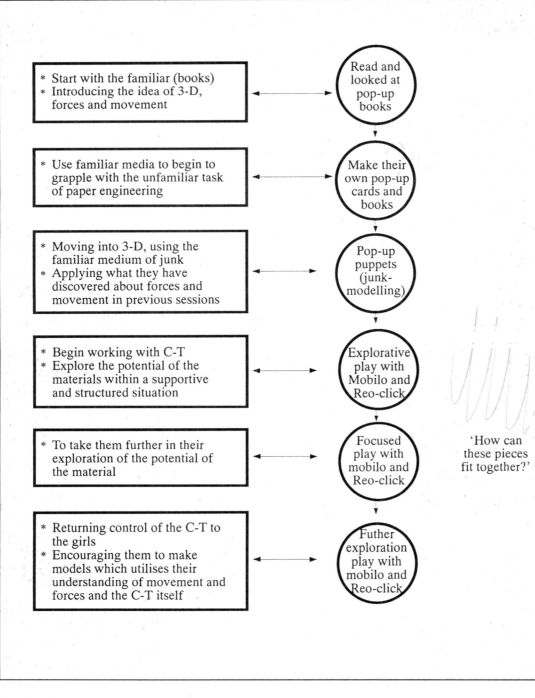

Aims:

Investigate types of materials
Investigate forces
Investigate types of movement
Investigate concepts of shape and space
Design and make
Practical problem solving/exploring possible solutions
Use measurement

* Start with the familiar (books)
* Introducing the idea of 3-D, forces and movement

Read and looked at pop-up books

* Use familiar media to begin to grapple with the unfamiliar task of paper engineering

Make their own pop-up cards and books

* Moving into 3-D, using the familiar medium of junk
* Applying what they have discovered about forces and movement in previous sessions

Pop-up puppets (junk-modelling)

* Begin working with C-T
* Explore the potential of the materials within a supportive and structured situation

Explorative play with Mobilo and Reo-click

* To take them further in their exploration of the potential of the material

Focused play with mobilo and Reo-click

* Returning control of the C-T to the girls
* Encouraging them to make models which utilises their understanding of movement and forces and the C-T itself

Futher exploration play with mobilo and Reo-click

'How can these pieces fit together?'

Classroom observations show that factors related to time and space can adversely affect girls' access to constructional activities. Below are four of the most common situations:

☐ Domination of materials and physical space by boys.

☐ Girls often marginalised or assuming a restrictive role in boy-girl groups.

☐ Girls have spent very little time playing with construction toys so may be limited in their approach and confidence.

☐ In any group activity, some children will be consistently dominant or active; others will be consistently passive or less active.

> **We need to develop deliberate strategies that ensure that girls have sufficient time and space for the task.**

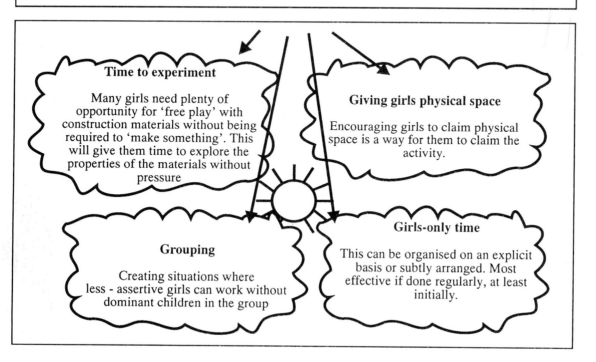

Time to experiment

Many girls need plenty of opportunity for 'free play' with construction materials without being required to 'make something'. This will give them time to explore the properties of the materials without pressure

Giving girls physical space

Encouraging girls to claim physical space is a way for them to claim the activity.

Grouping

Creating situations where less - assertive girls can work without dominant children in the group

Girls-only time

This can be organised on an explicit basis or subtly arranged. Most effective if done regularly, at least initially.

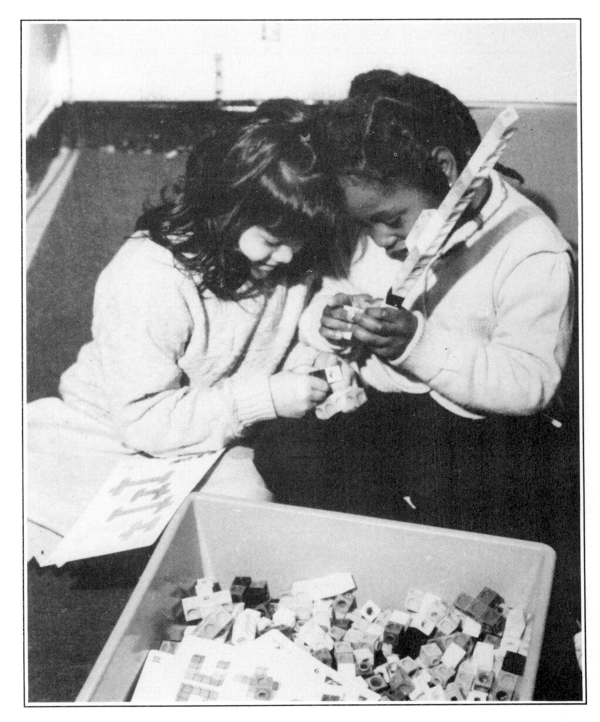

IV   Taking it apart and putting it back together again

If girls in your class are involved in constructional activities *but....*

☐ you feel their exploration of the potential of the medium is limited;

☐ you want to focus on a specific piece of learning (such as 'movement');

☐ you feel that lack of confidence and fear of making mistakes is restricting them...

Providing them with something to dismantle and reassemble could be a way forward.

Provide something for the girls to take apart and reassemble. This could be a model made out of a particular material; a part of a model (e.g. a hinge, something which rotates, spins etc.); or a real object. Knowing the component parts can help to 'demystify' the whole.

Encourage the girls to look at the structure as a whole and discuss what it does and how it works.

Encourage them to identify each component and its function as they dismantle it.

This idea can be developed into a game. The girls can make things for one another to take apart and put back together (the structures can be of varying complexity).

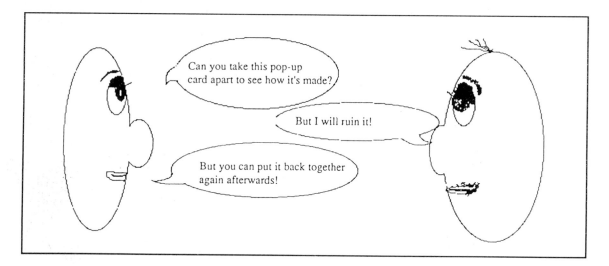

V   Copying

Providing a model or a picture of a model which can be copied can offer a 'way in' to constructional activities for girls who seem unwilling to make a start or don't know where to begin. It can offer something to focus on, the security of a definite goal and it can help remove the insecurity of an unknown medium. Also, copying is an activity many girls are comfortable with.

☐ This strategy, however, has limited use. Copying, in itself, doesn't ensure that the concepts or the medium are being explored.

Our research indicates that although girls often tend to be more fluent in their language development, they use the 'language of technology' less often and with less precision than do many boys.

Deliberate use of these words within a range of contexts can serve to clarify and familiarise the concepts and help girls to discuss and think through a construction process more accurately.

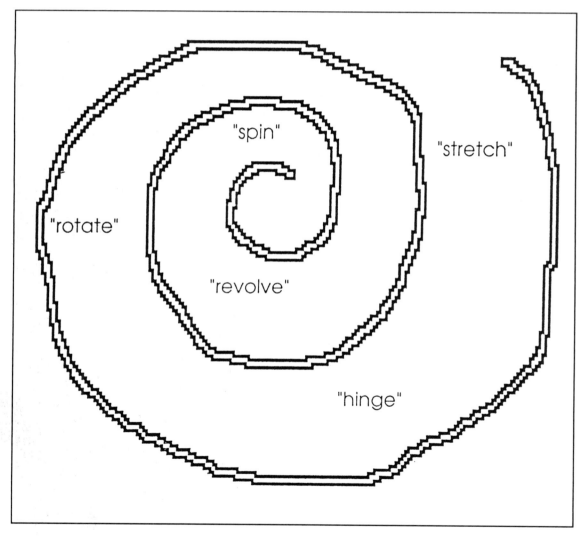

"spin"

"stretch"

"rotate"

"revolve"

"hinge"

When children have 'free choice', what they choose may be gender-related. Research indicates that girls and boys often favour quite different activities that develop very different skills and concepts — girls choosing activities with scope for social interplay and boys choosing constructional and active play.

What's on offer?

What activities are the children choosing between? One strategy is to set aside times when *all* the activities on offer in the classroom are technology-related.

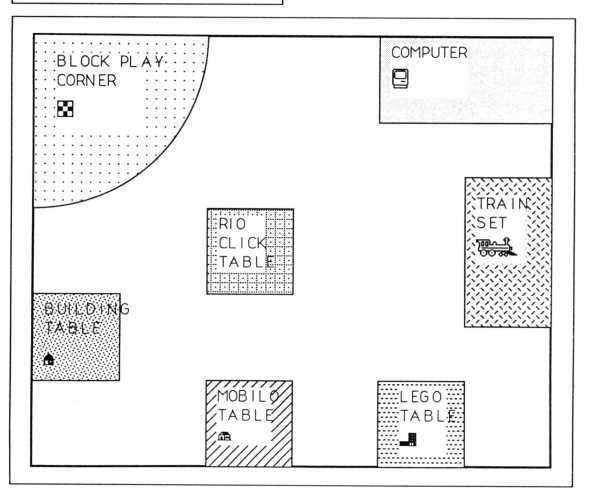

Even when girls do choose to play with construction toys, they may use the materials as a vehicle for social play instead of exploring the potential of the medium. For instance, lego is commonly used by girls to construct a rudimentary 'house' and then to play 'families'. One strategy is to remove the windows, doors, floor and 'play people' from the set.

Remove the 'Girl-bits'

There are many ways of presenting construction toys to children that avoid the 'house or car' model. For example, offer pictures or models of animals, pushchairs, prams, trolleys, patterns, playground, etc. These usually appeal to girls as well as boys and give more scope for developing constructional skills than do 'houses'.

SUGGEST ALTERNATIVES
TO HOUSE/CAR

REMOVE THE "GIRL-BITS"

- ☐ *Am I being supportive or pre-emptive?*

- ☐ *Is this necessary intervention — or un-wanted interference?*

- ☐ *What sort of role model am I providing?*

- ☐ *What messages am I giving about the value of various activities and their appropriateness for girls or boys through my involvement or lack of involvement?*

- ☐ *I am more confident and more 'at ease' in some activities than others?*

- ☐ *I've noticed myself watching (or mediating) the children who play with blocks and lego. But am I actively involved in other, non-constructional activities?*

Our evidence suggests that girls may be more concerned than boys with 'getting it right' and pleasing the teacher — and this can mean they are uncomfortable 'taking risks' when they approach unfamiliar activities. Exploring new materials involves trial and error. Too often we find girls 'opting out' at the point of uncertainty (while boys may often 'plunge in' regardless).

It's the role of the adult to encourage children to go further in their exploration and ease them over their 'opting out' points. But too much intervention can discourage initiative, undermine confidence and encourage dependency.

Remember — construction toys are usually 'free-choice' activities. This can mean they receive very little adult attention.

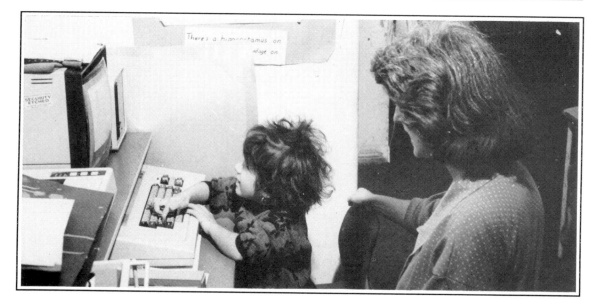

SECTION 3

Exploring Issues
INSET Ideas

I. Girls' Play? Boys' Play?
Investigating children's perceptions about play activities

Photographs of various activities on offer in early years classrooms (without any children present) can serve as a useful trigger for discussion or as a basis for interviewing young children about their play preferences, so helping to clarify gender differences. Use the photographs provided here or take some of your own empty classroom, to explore the perceptions of the girls and boys in your class.

Useful questions to ask the children:

☐ Do you play with this (re each photograph)?

☐ Who plays with it most?

☐ Who plays with it least?

☐ How do you use this? (What do you do/make?)

☐ What does..........................(fill in boy/girl names) do with it?

☐ Do you have this/do this at home?

☐ What do you like to play with most?

☐ What do you like to play with least?

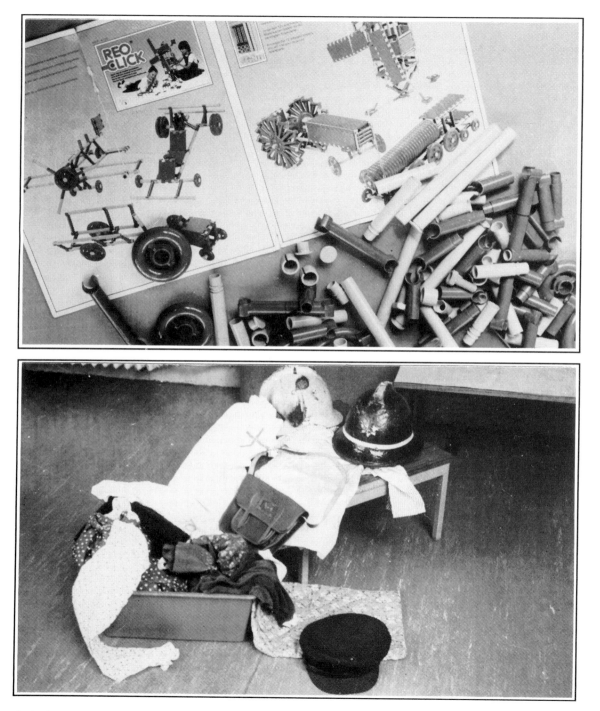

II. Classroom Observation

We know what we intend to be happening in our classrooms, but what else is going on? Many factors affect children's experience of school.

Deliberate classroom observation is one useful way of clarifying the different learning experiences children are having.

Observe your classroom (or swap classroom observations with another teacher for 'fresh eyes') to monitor:

☐ what children are choosing to play with

☐ how they are engaging in activities or using materials

☐ who uses what equipment and how often

☐ which activities are dominated by which groups of children

☐ how children interact around activities

☐ how far the differences you observe relate to gender.

Close classroom observation can bring to light many important issues which are central in identifying the educational needs of different children.

Observation can be broad or focused. It is often useful to begin with a non-specific brief and simply jot down whatever you notice for several sessions. Things that you've noted or that arise repeatedly in your observation can then become the focus for more detailed observation. We include some ideas for doing classroom observation.

---

a. Using photographs as an aid to Classroom Observation

Taking photographs is a quick and easy way of recording slices of classroom life.

They can be analysed later on, at your leisure.

We include some photographs (pp.00) which illustrate gender differences commonly observed in children's play choices and interactions. These can usefully be made a part of an INSET session to explore a range of related issues.

---

b. Focused Observation

Use the chart provided to help monitor the extent to which various activities are gender differentiated.

(Compare the outcomes with an analysis of what type of learning the various activities promote).

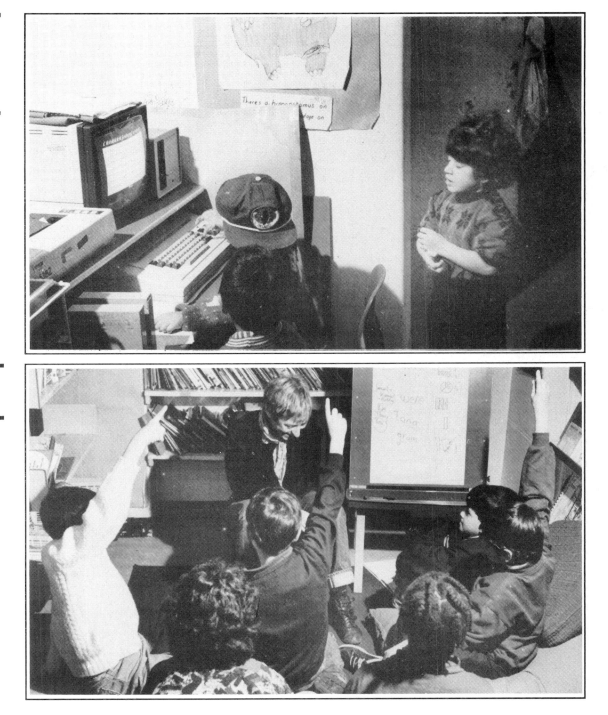

Monitoring use of various activities in early Years classrooms

Activity	Girls	Boys	How are the materials being used?	Teacher present?	COMMENTS

III. Analysing Activities

Early years classrooms are organised so that various play activities correlate to various curriculum areas and develop particular skills. Considering the central learning processes and intended education outcomes in relation to each activity/area on offer in the classroom can be a useful basis for monitoring the development of each child across the curriculum.

Compare the results of your classroom monitoring with this analysis to help clarify whether or not all children are getting the full range of educational experiences. This is particularly important in early years classrooms where 'free choice' is operating and children may be limiting their learning experiences through constantly making limited play choices.

AREA OF PROVISON	MAIN LEARNING PROCESSES INTENDED EDUCATION OUTCOMES OF EACH AREA
Outdoor Play	Develops:
Role Play (Home corner, dressing up…)	Develops:
Malleable Materials (eg. clay, dough…)	Develops:
Construction (lego, mobilo, wood…)	Develops:
Art and craft	Develops:
Literacy (book corner)	Develops:
Puzzle Activities	Develops:

IV. Analysing Classroom Organisation

Classroom organisation can have enormous impact on classroom dynamics. We have found it valuable to take time out to analyse the organisation of the classroom and the possibilities for re-organisation it.

Draw a plan of your classroom

Note the activities that are on offer at a given time

Show the arrangement of space

Indicate the placement of adults

Indicate time allocations of various activities

Examine your plans in terms of:

Messages about which activities are most valued

Gender polarisation in terms of use of space and equipment

Types of social interaction most likely to be found in the various areas

Plan a Reorganisation:

Project the impact your new plan would have on:

the use of space?

uptake of activities?

adult interventions?

group dynamics?

other considerations?

V. Hidden Messages

It is important to have a close look at our classrooms to analyse 'hidden' messages that children may be receiving. These, though unintentional, can be powerful and may be teaching the children gender 'norms' that interfere with their view of themselves as fully capable *and* caring people.

Resources, for example, give a strong 'message' about the world and what is the 'norm'. Too often they can reflect bias in terms of race and gender. For example, certain activities or jobs may appear to be either male or female domains. The people shown may be all or mostly white, and black people may be shown in very limited and even stereotypical contexts. The cultural context presented may be Eurocentric.

As we know, children readily absorb the images and 'norms' around them, which in turn can have an effect in determining children's areas of interest, goals and expectations. In this sense, hidden messages can influence pupil confidence, choices and performance across the curriculum. Too often girls and boys learn to value themselves, set their goals and pursue interests in very different ways.

Analyse your classroom and wider school environment to try to identify these hidden messages and how this could affect the children's self-image and aspirations:

Use of space:
what's available? who dominates? who's marginalised?

Books:
who does what? who is/isn't represented? how?

Visual images:
illustrations, posters, television...

Use of equipment acttivities:
to whom do different aspects of the classroom (or playground) 'belong'?

Adult role models:
how do children view adults' roles and positions within the school community?

School ethos:
assemblies, notices, values, assumptions, expectations...

VI. Analysing Children's Talk

It can be quite revealing to listen closely to children talking around an activity. The kind of talk taking place can highlight the kind of learning going on, the focus of the children's attention and the role of the adult. There are well-documented differences in the talk of girls and boys. Often, girls' talk indicates that social interaction or social play is their true focus and that the activity in secondary. Boys' talk may relate more directly to the activity they're engaged in and be more competitive in nature. In this way, girls and boys may be engaged in the same activities, yet focused quite differently and therefore undergoing different learning experiences.

Record children's conversations in your own classrooms or use the two we transcribed and include on the following pages — Water Play and Clay Play. Consider:

How are the children relating to each other?

Does the talk indicate a competitive or a collaborative approach?

Are the children concerned with seeking approval? (from other children? from the adult?)

Are the children concerned with getting what they want in the situation?

Do they listen well? or are they more concerned with what they want to say?

Other social aspects of the conversation?

Is the talk interactive? or are the children preoccupied and single-minded?

Water Play

Four boys and Nursery Nurse student.

Aim of activity: to develop concepts related to floating and sinking.
Variety of objects to experiment with included corks, blocks of wood, stones etc.

(Children playing with wooden blocks in the water. Some dispute over one of the blocks of wood.)

B1:   I'll tell him when I've finished.

B2:   Put it on the water.

B1:   Is it hot water?

Adult: No, it's nice and warm for you.

B1:   Hey, want to splash it (his floating wooden block.).. splash this water... EEE-AAH,EE-AAH, [splashes water with his hands.]

Adult: Do you want a plastic bowl?

B2:   No-oo- oo

B1:   And I want...what is this for?...And this is gonna be on his head. [Puts wooden block on B2's head.]

B1:   [Tries to take B2's block.]

B2:   (screams) *NO!*

Adult::   When he's finished he's going to let you have it.

B1:   Yeah.

B3:   I want this one. I want those. I want this thing (points to B4's block).

Adult: No, you're going to have one of Jerry's aren't you? When Jerry's finished...

B3:   No. I want that one...

Adult: You'll have to wait.

B3:   I want a long one.

Adult: A long one.

B3:   I don't want to wait 'til he's finished.

Adult: No, when Jerry's finished 'cos Jerry's got two.

B3:   I want this one.

Adult: Well, Jerry's got that one.

    [Children continue for a minute or so with no discernible comments.]

B1:   I'll make it float.

B3:   I've got none of this one. I've got none of this one. I want a long, long one. I want that long one, alright? Mary! I want that long one.

Adult: Victor's using that one. You have this one in a minute, Jerry!

Jerry: Float this one and then let(??) have a go, alright?

B3:   I want his one. I want a long, long one.

B2:   You're the next one, alright?

B3:   Mary, I want that long one [splashing water makes tape indistinct for next 30 secs].

B2:   I'll give it to you and then you give it to him, alright?

B2:   You're the next one, alright?

B3:   Mary, I want that long one.

[Splashing water makes tape indistinct for next 30 secs].

B2: I'll give it to you and then you give it to him, alright?

B1: No. No! Give it to him... *oh!* He splashed my one! Stop it! Stop it!

[B3: continues to make waves]

B1: Stop. Oi! Stop it... He don't make my one float. Oi! Stop it!... He don't stop.

Adult: Victor, wait a minute, love. Making waves?

B2: I found this under the water.

Adult: Oh yeah. A bottle top... Let me see if I can make this piece of wood float.

B2: No, don't (as one of the others tries to take his wooden block)...

B3: Johnny! You'll make it fall down!

B2: What is it?

Adult: It's a rock. It usually sinks. See if you can make it float.

BG: I'll make it float.

[He puts the rock in the water and it simply sinks. The others watch and laugh as it sinks.]

B3: Why? (i.e. why did it sink?)

Adult: Because it's heavy isn't it? This floats (a cork) and the wood floats because they're very light.

B1: Splash! Splash!

B2: That's dangerous in the water.

B3: I want to play with that.

B1: I don't want it anymore, I'm going outside.

Adult: Going outside?

[Two boys (B1 and B2) and the adult leave the water tray.

B3 balances four corks on a block of wood. The adult returns]

Adult: Will it float like that?

[B4 slaps the water to make waves.]

Adult: Will it float?

B3: Look! it will...

[B4 continued to make waves.]

B3: Hey... watch... see? Look this going un (sic) the water. This going down the water (the wooden blocks etc sink).

B4: It's too big...

[Children splash the water. Tape indistinct for minute.]

B3: Look, look, look, it's coming out! (A cork kept bouncing up)

Adult: Let's see if I can float this...

[Child floats a piece of wood which, when he pushes it away from the side, returns because of the water movement.]

B3: Wheee! (as wood returns).

B4: The water's sticky.

Adult: Sticky?

B4: The water on my hands is sticky.

Adult: The water sticks to your hands?

B4: Yeah... The water won't come off... I'm shaking (shakes his hands).

Adult: It won't come off, it still sticks.

B4: Why? It makes your hands go sticky.

Adult: It makes your hands get wet and they stay wet for a long time

[Children splash the water and look at their hands.]

Adult: That was a big splash.

Clay Play

Four girls and an adult — the four girls busy moulding and shaping the clay. The adult had already made a thumb pot.

Girl A: This is a bum.

Adult: You made it with your thumb?

Girl A: No. it's a bum.

Adult: Did you come with us to see Ray making pots and he stuck his thumb in and then he pressed round the sides to make a pot?

Girl A: Sarah went.

Adult: Sarah went, that's right and what was the pot called? Do you remember?

Girl A: And Emma went.

Adult: What was its name? It was called a...?

Girl B: (indistinct).

Adult: That's right, like Little Jack Horner.

[The adult goes up to deal with something. The children at the table notice me and the tape recorder and become wary!]

Girl B: I'm doing a little cake, for Daniel. You don't know who Daniel is, he's my friend and I'm gonna make a cake for him.

Girl C: (to Girl B) Are you my friend?

[Adult returns.]

Girl B: I'm making Thomas the Tank Engine and it's for Daniel.

Adult: That's nice, it's his favourite, isn't it? Do you remember on his birthday he got four Thomas the Tank Engine cards? (To Girl D) Are you going to make something to put in your pot?

Girl A: I'm going to make a birthday cake.

Girl B: This is a baby bird... This is a child's... This is a baby bird.

[2 minutes of indistinct tape.]

Girl B: Got to make some legs

Adult: Shall we put the pea in this? What's that? Something for the baby to eat? Do you think baby birds eat peas?

Girl C: No, they eat nuts.

Adult: Nuts. We put some nuts out for the birds.

Girl B: No, they eat bread.

Adult: Oh Lawrence I forgot about your finger. (Adult leaves the table.)

Girl A: Why have you got big eggs?

Girl B: I know what she's making, I know.

Girl A: A cup.

Girl B: No guess, guess.

Girl A: I don't care.

Girl B: Huh! Huh!

(indistinct tape)

Girl A: Guess what I'm making.

Girl B: You don't know what this... what I'm gonna make.

Girl C: You don't know what I'm making.

Girl B: A worm. I know what it is.

Girl C: What?

Girl B: Worms are yukky.

Girl A: Yes!

Girl C: It's a snake.

Girl B: Oh well, I don't care I'm never going to be anybody's friend.

Girl C: I never heard you say anything naughty.

I like... I still like you but no-one else,

Girl B: Ugh!

Girl A: You won't have no... anyone have no lots of friends.

Girl B: Well I've got lots of friends who go to different schools and I like them better than all my school friends 'cept Claudia, Claudia is my friend.

Girl C: We have to like one another, we have to...

Girl B: Everybody has got to be Claudia's friend... only not you (to Girl A) only you not like Claudia. So everyone likes Claudia 'cept you... naughty girl.

Girl C: You've got to be anybody's friend

Girl A: I'm just going to be (?) friend.

[Girl B begins beating the clay and hits her finger.]

Girl B: Ouch!

Girl C: Did that hurt?

Girl A: My mum'll tell me off.

Girl B: She won't tell me off.

Girl C: No, she'll tell Charlotte off won't she? you're my friend aren't you?

Girl A: Now I'm not your friend any more Claudia cos you're just being friends with her.

Girl B: My cousin... Charlotte, she likes... she's older than me... she's older than you... she's taller than you...

Girl A: And my brother might get you and stand on you, Claudia.

Girl C: And I might not come to see you any-more.

[For about two minutes the children ignore each other until an adult approaches the table.]

Girl C: Charlotte doesn't like me anymore!

Adult: What have you been saying Charlotte?

Girl B: Well, they these two like together and they two don't like me and Sophie say she don't like me.

Adult: That's not like you to say you don't like anybody, we usually play together don't we? I don't really want you to say you don't like someone else, OK? It's nice to have all different friends and play with them at different times. Then you don't hurt people's feelings, if you say you don't like someone sometimes it really hurts them and it's not nice.

Girl C: And it's not fair.

Adult: It's not, fair no.

> **Do you find that the boys take over the science equipment?**
>
> **Do girls choose construction activities less often than boys?**
>
> **Are the girls developing mechanical manipulation and spatial skills?**
>
> **How do boys' games and girls' games exercise control over space in the playground? Does it matter?**
>
> **Are the boys and girls learning the same skills?**
>
> **What activities take up most space and who does them?**

Here are some specific areas you may wish to focus on for further investigation:

Collaboration

Entitlement:
When using the same materials for different purposes, is one usage more productive than others?

Does the girls' need for social play dominate their learning activities?

Do girls stick to a 'prescription'?

Are they overly concerned with pleasing the teacher?

Are boys better at rule-making and rule-breaking? Is it more a feature of their approach to play? Do they tend to improvise more?

How does minding whether you are wrong most affect learning?

If construction activities come down to houses vs cars, what does this mean for the scope of the activity?

Do girls accept boys' evaluation of them as 'useless' (e.g. at football, lego)?

What are the parent's attitudes?
Are boys more interested in process?
Are girls more interested in product?

What does this imply for their learning experiences?

Where do the models for their play come from?

Other Reading

Browne, N. (ed.) (1991) Science and Technology in the Early Years, OUP

Catton, John (1985) *Ways and means: the craft, design and technology education of girls.* (Developing the curriculum for a changing world) (Schools Council programme 3) York: Longman

Cary, Caroline (1990) *Jo's garage.* Pictures by Gerald Hawksley, Treehouse

Claire, Hilary, Jo Melhuish and Anne Waldon (1990) *Dragons & milkcrates: design technology in the first school: contexts and strategies for supporting girls.* London: Ealing Education Service

Dickenson, Mary (1981) *Alex's bed.* Pictures by Charlotte Firmin, London: Scholastic

Equal Opportunities Commission(1983) *Equal opportunities in craft, design & technology* , EOC

Lloyd, B. and Dureen, G. (1992) *Gender Identities and Education — The Impact of Starting School*, Harvester-Wheatsheaf

London Borough of Brent, CDSU (1986) *Breaking the circuit: girls, boys & electronics: a research project*, Brent

London Borough of Brent, (1988) CDSU *Design it, Use It.*

Milman, Val (1984) *Teaching technology to girls.* Coventry: Elm Bank Teachers' Centre

Myers, K. (ed) (1992) *Genderwatch! — after the Education Reform Act*, Cambridge University Press

Stewart, Carole (1983) *Deanne and Sue go building.* Pictures by Deanne Taylor, Sydney: Hale and Iremongar

Tutchell, e. (ed) (1991) *Dolls and Dungarees — Gender Issues in the Primary School Curriculum*, OUP